DEVELOPING PEOPLE

TOP 10 TIPS FOR NEW & MIDDLE MANAGERS

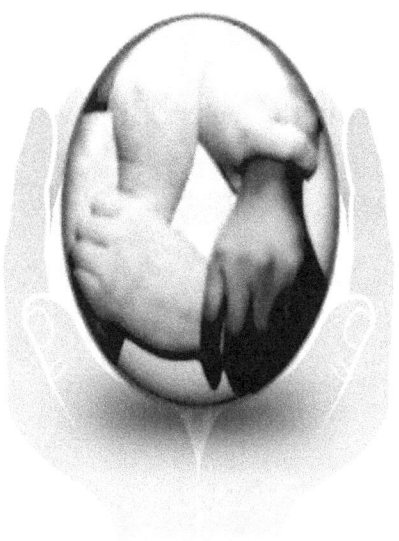

Unleash the potential in your people!

AUDREY EZEKWESILI

WWW.FACILITATE4ME.COM
April 2012

Dedication

To my dear Ben, Ebony, Isabelle & Sam. I lack the words to succinctly express how much you mean to me, so for once, I shall just stay quiet ....☺!

Contents

DEDICATION 2

CONTENTS 3

ACKNOWLEDGEMENTS 5

ACKNOWLEDGEMENTS 5

DEVELOPING PEOPLE 6

INTRODUCTION 6

1 12

DEVELOPING PEOPLE IS ABOUT MAKING AN "INVESTMENT" 12

2 14

I IS FOR INVEST IN YOURSELF 14

3 27

N IS FOR KNOW YOUR STAFF 27

4 35

V IS FOR REINVENT WITH THE TIMES 35

5 40

E IS FOR EMPOWER YOUR PEOPLE .... AND YOURSELF 40

6 44

S IS FOR SLAVERY IS OFFICALLY OVER! 44

7 47

T IS FOR TALENT MANAGEMENT 47

8 54

M IS FOR MOTIVATE YOUR STAFF 54

9 62

E IS FOR EMPLOY THE RIGHT PEOPLE 62

10 66

N IS FOR NETWORK, NETWORK, NETWORK! 66

11 71

T IS FOR THINK CREATIVELY 71

12 .... **75**

AND NOT FORGETTING TO...COMMUNICATE, COMMUNICATE, COMMUNICATE!
.... **75**

13 .... **83**

CONCLUSION.. **83**

BIBLIOGRAPHY **85**

Acknowledgements

I am reminded of an old African proverb which states that it takes a whole village to train a child. In my case, I have had one hell of a mighty village behind me with too many people to name individually. I will therefore humbly beg their forgiveness as I modestly summarise their contributions.

To:
- All my colleagues and friends over the years who have contributed to my development across a variety of business sectors and industries;
- All my confidants who have given me the confidence to rise above my numerous fears & challenges;
- All my Managers, Mentors and Coaches over the years who have allowed me to model them and have created opportunities for me whenever possible;
- Facilitate4me service providers who have generously and unreservedly continued to offer their time and advice long after our official contractual relationships ended; and
- Ifeoma, Paul, Alan, Paul, Chinwe, Philip, Ben, Ebony, Isabelle & Sam who provided valuable feedback to this book,

I say "Thank you" so very, very much.

Last, but my no means least, I am deeply, deeply indebted to the Almighty Father ...for absolutely everything!

Developing People

Introduction

In November 2011, the Personnel Today published an article under the heading *"Bad management costing business billions"* in which it quoted a survey by the Chartered Management Institute (CMI) which concluded that bad management could be costing UK businesses more than £19 billion every year. According to the report, the worst management practices (which incidentally relate to developing people) included unclear communication, lack of support, micro management and lack of direction of their staff.

After over twenty years in management, across a variety of industries and sectors, I can honestly say that the result of the survey doesn't come as a surprise to me. I would also surmise that although the survey is UK based, the same results could easily be replicated across the world.

In defence of managers however, I do not believe that this failure is deliberate.

In my experience, managers on the whole are intelligent and business savvy. Most tend to be on top of their business or departmental goals and the actions that they need to achieve their goals. Most can quote, off head, the performance increase and decrease on the Profit and Loss accounts and any other performance tracking measures that they have and most can tell you the business reasons and justifications for their performance. They know this because it is their <u>core</u> business, as managers to know.

They also know how to access a business resource to help them explain the bits that they don't know. Such resources could be the views of their customers (through direct contact or customer surveys), previous departmental reports and also other business colleagues and peers. If all these fail, they also have access to the business sections of the media (Newspapers, TV and Radio news items, and dedicated business programmes) as additional resources. Everyone recognises that as a manager or head of department, the bottom line profit is ultimately what you are measured against.

So where does developing people feature in the priority of Managers?

> People are our greatest assets

Every manager, head of department, or leader worth their salt would tell you that even though their business is made up of Systems (IT technology) and Processes, that it is infact People which are the key assets in their businesses. This mantra is well known. However, when push comes to shove and the reality of delivering business profits starts to bite, particularly in a hard economic climate, many Managers and employees alike report that People considerations are often relegated to the back of the queue. Leadership training and development initiatives are cut in the quest to save money and organisation restructures and downsizing initiatives are implemented in order to swiftly (and magically) drive efficiencies. For the lucky employee who still has a job after a restructure, comes the expectation that they should take on the additional tasks and roles of the people who were let go, and automatically hit the ground running to deliver, often with minimum or no support, minimum communication, minimum direction and minimum development and training.

> The life of a Manager can be a lonely one

As a Manager, I have often felt the uneasy emotion of being stuck between a rock and a hard place. On the one hand, I am torn between the desire to deliver value for my department/ organisation in the shortest timescale possible knowing full well that this was the best way to demonstrate the Return on Investment in my staff, whilst on the other hand, being forced to acknowledge that for my staff to deliver the outputs (services and products) required, I needed to invest a significant amount of time and effort and indeed money, on developing them. This is time and money that many managers often claim not to have.

> If it weren't for people, my department would be more profitable!

I have often heard some of my colleagues lament that if it weren't for people and their unpredictability, uncertainty and inefficiencies, their department would be far more profitable. For these Managers, the consistency and reliability of IT systems are comforting and much more valuable than people. On one level, I can see their viewpoint. Figure 1 below depicts the popular representation of People, Processes and Systems in an Organisation in a manner which suggests that it is <u>logically</u> possible to drive a profitable business with a minimum investment in people - so long as processes and systems are in place.

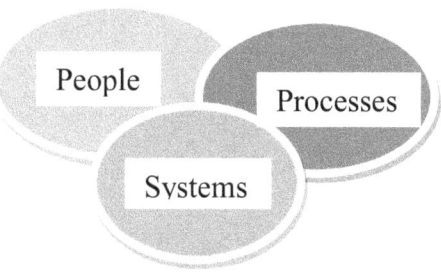

Figure 1

The problem is that the **Figure 1** depiction is inaccurate. People, Systems and Processes are not really replicated in business in equal measures. The simple truth is that no matter what you deliver or produce in your business and how you deliver it, you need your people to specify what you need to do, how you need to do it (processes) and to drive the tools and equipment (systems) that you need to deliver it with. Also, given that all businesses exist to deliver a product or service of sustainable value to people as individuals (customers) or people in other businesses, you ultimately need your people to understand what these customers need and how to be responsive to them. The bottom line then is that the "People" element of a business has a much larger ratio of the People, Processes and

Systems equation than is usually depicted and, in reality, looks more like Figure 2.

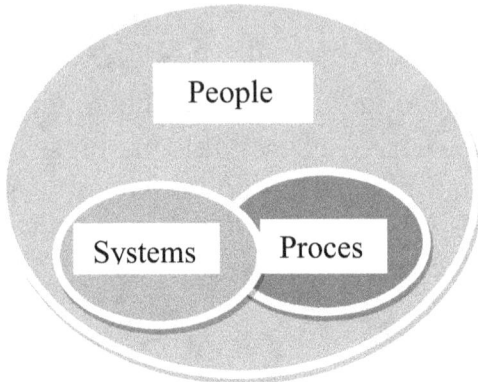

Figure 2

Given the large emphasis placed on People for the survival of an Organisation or Business, it stands to reason that care must be taken to place this responsibility in the hands of great people only.

Great people in business are developed - usually by great Managers and Leaders. Ultimately, therefore, the most important task that a Manager has is to develop his people to drive the bottom line profitability. This is a bit like the children's story of the Farmer, the Goose and the Golden Egg. Whereas the golden eggs laid by the goose are extremely profitable to the farmer and are indeed the products which have the potential to make him wealthy, failure of the farmer to look after the well-being of the goose ultimately proves to be disastrous as it dries up the source of the farmer's wealth.

> Developing People is about making an
> **INVESTMENT**

Looking after the well being of the golden goose is akin to developing people with the Manager as the Farmer. Often the Manager will be tempted to take short cuts to get to the bottom line profits. This is disastrous in the long run, and will often prove costly, as depicted in the CMI survey.

Developing people is a necessary INVESTMENT for the future of your business and in this book, I cover the key elements of this investment in a simple non technical language. The book is designed to answer the top 10 popular questions that I have received over the years mostly from new and middle managers. It is a practical book with practical examples from my experience that anyone can relate and refer to again and again. On occasions, I have referred to pieces of development theories which are currently in the public domain just to illustrate the relationship between the theories and their realistic applications in the workplace.

 I do not profess to be an expert in developing people. I have had lots of successes and made lots of mistakes and I have tried as much as possible to illustrate ample examples of both in this book as I feel that both provide important lessons.

We are all in this together and if this book works, then you will find yourself relating to it as if a pocket book coach. If it doesn't work, at least you would know to try something else. In either case, I could definitely welcome feedback via www.faciliate4me.com

1

DEVELOPING PEOPLE IS ABOUT MAKING AN "INVESTMENT"

> *"Faith is taking the first step, even when you don't see the whole staircase.*
>
> Martin Luther King Jnr

It has become more and more apparent that to develop people is to make a strategic investment in the realisation of a business' objectives. The smart business manager /owner knows that it is not just about the amount of investment made, but in the type of investment.

For the manager the word "INVESTMENT" is broken down into the following:

- I is for ....Invest in yourself
- N is for .... kNow your staff
- V is for .... reinVent with the times
- E is for ....Empower your people....and ultimately yourself
- S is for .... Slavery is officially over!
- T is for............Talent Management

- M is for..........Motivate for people
- E is for ....Employ & Engage the right people
- N is for ....Network, Network, Network!
- T is for .... Think Creatively

The following chapters in this book deal with each aspect of the people "INVESTMENT" in turn.

2

I is for INVEST IN YOURSELF

> *"A person whom many have gathered to see does not come out covered in soot"*
>
> Nigerian (Igbo) proverb

The Nigerian proverb above is a great way to illustrate the first key criteria in developing people. Put simply, charity begins at home. It is vital that a manager, who aspires to develop people, should first of all invest in developing himself as a "People Manager". [1]

A team is generally perceived as a reflection of the capabilities of their manager. The manager sets the temperature for the performance of his team and its individual members. As such, poor management skills will often breed poor team behaviours either consciously or subconsciously.

Years ago, I was fortunate enough to coach a person who was experiencing difficult relationships with his team

---

[1] The term "People Manager" is used in this book to differentiate a person who manages people from one who manages processes or systems. Different skills and competencies are required for these management roles

members which was affecting his performance. John (not his real name obviously), found his opinions being ignored in team meetings and his work contributions being belittled, with every single mistake highlighted for all to see.

Early in our coaching relationship, I quickly established that John's treatment from his fellow colleagues was an exact replica of the treatment he was receiving from his line manager (who was also the line manager of his colleagues). John's manager frequently belittled him openly in team meetings and in the open office plan.

Unsurprisingly, the more this happened, the more John lost his confidence and the more his performance suffered which gave his manager more reason to declare, to any who would hear, that he was useless. As time went on John was dismayed to discover that even the peers that he was once close to and enjoyed healthy working relationships with, for many years prior to the appointment of the line manager, now treated him as a leper. Whilst some openly sneered at him whenever their Manager humiliated him, others appeared clearly uncomfortable with this but failed to assist John in any way or to speak on his behalf.

As stated earlier, the manager rightly or wrongly sets the temperature or the yardstick of acceptable behaviour in a team and a 'pack' or "herd" mentally ensures whenever a Manager continuously brays for a team member's blood.

John finally decided to invest in himself by seeking the services of a coach when he recognised himself exhibiting some of his Line Manager's behaviours with his own direct team. To him, that was a wake- up call that something had to be done. As he put it, he didn't want his team to suffer from having an inept manager just as he was doing!

> "You must become the change that you want to see in others"
> - Ghandi

As a manager, investing in yourself is about 5 main things:-
1) Appraising yourself
2) Getting others to honestly appraise you
3) Being clear as to why you are a Manager <u>and</u> what you wish to achieve from your management <u>assignment</u>
4) Understanding your gaps, challenges and/or barriers
5) Coaching and being coached! Mentoring and being mentored!

1. Appraise yourself

For years, I struggled with the activity of appraising myself as it resonated the more formal and often complicated annual appraisal systems found in organisations which, by their very nature are (a) infrequent, (b) regimented and (c) implied that something negative must be found about you, predominately to justify the resultant performance rating (and subsequent) performance related pay you would be awarded for the year.

I am not alone in this view.

I know many colleagues who treat this "appraise yourself" activity with the same trepidation. As a manager, I have seen such intense emotions about appraisals result in one or two behaviour types from colleagues, staff and managers alike:-

- A tendency to over inflate your qualities, highlighting all the strengths and either ignoring or completely denying any weaknesses or development areas or
- A tendency to bury one's head in the sand and develop complete apathy over the whole appraisal process. I have heard people say such things as "management will decide whatever they want, regardless of whatever you say you have achieved"

Either way, both reactions are unhealthy and completely overlook the excellent assistance that a regular self appraisal or self assessment can afford to anyone who wants to invest in their development, growth and success. So, as a line manager, I suggest that the first thing you need to do is to set the management temperature and regularly and honestly assess your skills and competencies as a People Manager. This doesn't have to be complicated. I recommend any of the following 3 self assessment tools which I have found to be the most valuable for me and which can also be extended to your team members as you desire.

1.1 Appraise yourself: Assess your values

Research abound which tell us that all human behaviours are motivated by either pain or pleasure values. People decide on what to do dependent on whether their action will move them away from feeling pain or move them towards gaining something pleasurable. We are told that most people, when faced with an activity which has the potential to get them pleasure if they do one thing (e.g. investing their last £1,000 on the possibility/probability of getting a £5,000 windfall in the outcome of the investment) or pain if they failed (e.g. not being able to afford the purchase of the £1,000 piece of jewellery they promised their spouse), will choose to do the activity which moves them away from the pain- no matter how unlikely that pain was! In this case, the spouse gets the jewellery most times!

In the context of the work environment and developing yourself, it is always good to understand what values you hold most high as a manager/leader and why. What values or emotional state would you do more to achieve, and what would you do more to escape from? Is it more important, for example, for you to empower your staff to make their own decisions or would you prefer that they do exactly what you want them to do and in exactly the same manner that you want them to do it?
If the latter, I suggest that people management may not be the right path for you. Perhaps a role in systems or process management might be better suited to your values…and a lot less stressful.

1.2. Appraise yourself: What do you enjoy doing and what are you good at?

This assessment tool is very simple and is based on the fact that we all have things, tasks, activities that we:-

- A - Enjoy doing and are good at
- B - Enjoy doing but aren't so good at...yet
- C - Don't enjoy doing but will do a good job if we have to
- D - Don't enjoy doing and aren't good at doing either.

Once this mapped out on a grid as in Figure 3, an interesting story emerges.

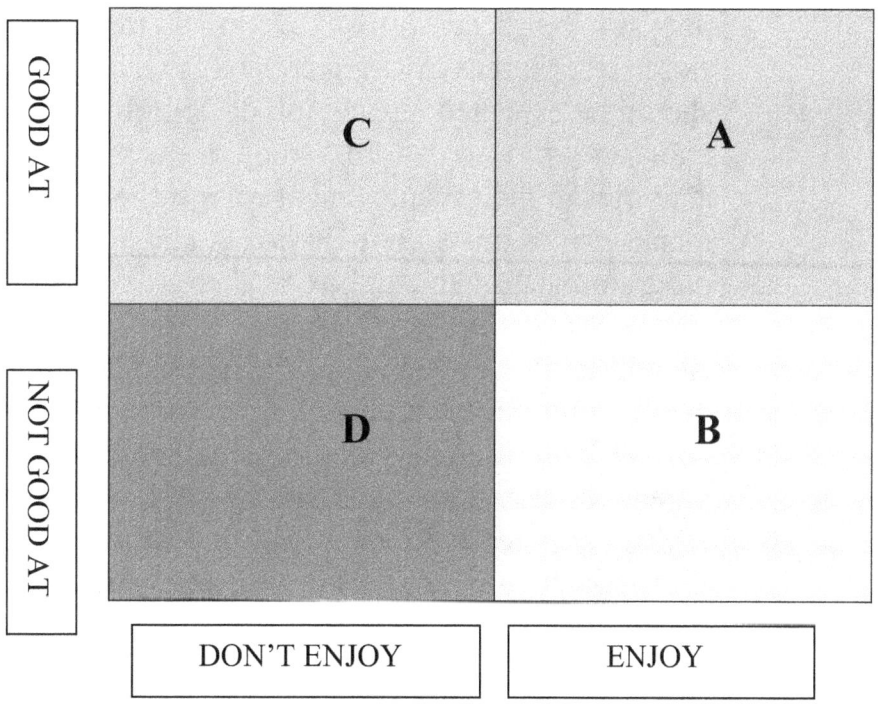

Figure 3 – Enjoyment Assessment Grid

When you complete the Enjoyment Assessment Grid, take care to do this by concentrating on specific *tasks* and *activities* and <u>not</u> roles. So, for example, project management is a role and should therefore not be listed in the grid whereas planning, controlling, monitoring, budgeting, communicating for example are all legitimate *activities* within project management which you may enjoy to varying degrees and therefore may be spread out across the various boxes in the grid accordingly.

In truth, you will find is that virtually all roles in your workplace contain a majority of the same activities or tasks which you have listed in the grid. However, the differentiator is the *degree* to which each activity or task is expected to be exercised in a specific role in order for the person to be successfully executing their role. So, for example, whereas giving feedback is an activity which should be expected in each job description or role, a manager will find that this is one of the most *essential* activities in their management role. If therefore a line manager lists this activity in box A and a Computer programmer lists this in box D, there is no need to panic.

As a Line/ People Manager, my recommendation is to avoid getting involved in activities listed in box 'D' at all costs. If you find that you have listed core activities or objectives related to managing people in your organisation in this box, please do yourself and your team a favour and find another role more rewarding and which plays to your strengths!
Likewise, the same sentiment goes to activities listed in box 'C'. People are *human* beings and not robots or processes or machinery. So, if you do not really really enjoy managing people, delivering through people, encouraging and motivating people, mentoring and coaching people and getting a huge amount of satisfaction and pride from the fact that a person whom you have been training up for the past few years has been internally headhunted by another department and promoted to a

www.facilitate4me.com

higher post, then, please, be good to yourself and find a role that doesn't involve managing or developing people. It is a tough and often thankless exercise and sometimes you will feel that you have taken 2 steps forward and 1.5 steps backwards.

This brings me to items listed in boxes 'A' and 'B' of the Enjoyment Assessment Grid. If you have listed such activities as performance management, having difficult conversations with people, coaching, mentoring, rewarding, , facilitating, developing people, giving praise, giving challenging and constructive feedback, hiring, firing, restructuring, change management, managing successes, managing grievances, providing on the job development opportunities, stakeholder management, selling your team, empowering your team, conflict resolution etc in these boxes...you are clearly mad! However, at least you are travelling on the right bus lane! The challenge you now have is to make sure that you are not just on the right bus lane but on the right bus and that you are picking up the right passengers and understanding their needs and aspirations and helping them to achieve these whilst you and them meet the requirements of the bus company that pays your respective salaries.

"Don't ask yourself what the world needs, ask yourself what makes you come alive. And then go and do that. Because what the world needs is people who are alive" - Howard Thurman

1.3. Appraise yourself: Asses and build up your Emotional Intelligence

My first management assignment over 20 years ago was as a graduate manager in charge of a team of 6 people of various ages and backgrounds, in one of the most prestigious organisations in the UK.

I was young, intelligent, well educated, enthusiastic, up for the challenge, ambitious and petrified!

I was managing a team of people with varying capabilities and my job was to deliver my department's objectives, motivate my team and develop a variety of management skills to further my career.

They knew I was 'green[2]' in every way- both operationally and managerially, but there was a certain amount of respect they had for me.

For my part, I was determined to prove that I was in charge. I was determined to change things and regardless of whether they had been doing the same activity for years, there was always room for improvement- whether they liked it or not.

Needless to say, I made mistakes.

Mistake number 1 was that I didn't invest in building the relevant rapport and relationship with my team which would allow them to follow me willingly rather than me pushing them.

Mistake number 2 was in thinking that all my team members were like me, quick, hungry, ambitious and willing to take on new challenges. I also hadn't accounted for the fact that people have different learning styles. So after I became visibly frustrated at a staff member who failed to grasp the basics of a new process that I was

---

[2] "Green" here refers to the level of my inexperience.

introducing on the spot, she pulled me aside and said, *"Please don't get angry but realise that not everyone is as intelligent as you"*. I was humbled. Up to that time, I hadn't even considered myself as being *particularly* intelligent. As far as I was concerned, what I was introducing was "common sense" and surely <u>anyone</u> could see and grasp it!

Looking back on it, I can honestly say that I wasn't a great manager and I didn't particularly enjoy managing people either. It was the means to an end. I was ambitious and being a manager was the right path for an ambitious employee.

Fast forward a couple of years later and I learnt about Emotional intelligence (EI)[3] and learnt that there is a BIG difference between EI and IQ. What I had in my early management career was IQ which was higher (much higher) than my EI. Now, I am proud to say that the reverse is the case!

As a People Manager, use any of the tools readily available on the internet to assess your emotional intelligence as this plays a much greater importance in your role. Do something about developing and increasing this.

2. Get others to appraise you

Investing in yourself also means understanding how others perceive you and acknowledging any blind spots that you may have when it comes to your prowess as a People

---

[3] Emotional Intelligence reference to the following competencies: Self Awareness, Self Management, Social Awareness and Relationship.

Manager. Again there are many tools that you can use for this including the formal 360 degree feedback mechanisms to the more informal one to one feedback. The most important thing is that you ask the right people for feedback and give them the permission to be open and honest with you without any fear that you will hold it against them. You also need to be brave as you might hear something which you weren't expecting. No matter how painful the feedback, ask yourself, isn't it far better that you know the specific areas that you need to develop in to be a better manager than continuing to wallow in your ignorance?

3. Be clear as to why you are a Manager <u>and</u> what you wish to achieve from your management "<u>assignment</u>"

One of the problems that line managers face is that often they get promoted into the management role as a "reward" for having achieved great success as technical or process Managers. For some strange reason, we continue in the UK to believe that every high performing employee either wants to line manage people and/ or has to be good at managing people. Neither is true. Indeed, in my experience, the managers who have been the most guilty of micro managing, not giving direction and not supporting their staff have often been people who have reluctantly taken up the role of people management as a promotion and /or who mistakenly thought that the same competencies that have earned them the promotion from their technical or none line management roles are exactly the same competencies that are needed in the People / Line management role.

I do not blame anyone for this sorry state. What I do expect though is that such managers stand up and be counted - either by proactively seeking to invest in specific tailored development interventions for themselves that are relevant for their new role or simply influencing *their* organisation and line managers that they add far better value to the organisation in senior technical and /or non line management positions

The other mistake that managers make is to regard the management status as a permanent one - a right of passage if you will. This therefore means that even when they realise that it is not the right path for you (for whatever reason) or indeed the right time for them, their perceived status is so tied up with it that any move away from this path is perceived as a failure by their peers, team and themselves.

For this reason, I recommend adopting an "assignment" mindset which means that you regard your current management role as an *assignment* which is temporary in nature and which you can change and adapt dependant on a variety of things including your and your organisation's requirement. Indeed that you are flexible enough to do this a huge string to your bow as will be discussed in the chapter on **"V is for reinVent yourself with the times"**

With your *"assignment"* mindset, give yourself permission to regularly refer to and update your Enjoyment Assessment Grid in Figure 3 anytime you wish to embark on a new assignment. If the new assignment does not align with what you enjoy doing and are good at or want to improve upon, then please try another assignment and still have your head help up high!

4. Understand your gaps, challenges and/or barriers

The output of appraising yourself, getting others to appraise you and adopting an assignment mindset should lead you to a better understanding of your priority development areas. The first development area should be the need for you to let go of the detail and move instead towards supporting or facilitating your people to the detail work themselves. . In other words, you need to elevate yourself to delivering through your people and applying the right and most appropriate leadership tools and style to get the best out of them regardless of their level of competence.

5. Coach and be coached! Mentor and be mentored!

Depending on your gaps and development priorities, there are a variety of development interventions that can be tailored specifically for you as a manager. Do your research and see what is most realistic and what you will find most effective. Unfortunately, there is no "one size fits all" as everyone is an individual. Popular activities include on the job development, coaching and mentoring, bespoke leadership development activities, networking, seminars, professional accreditations.

One of the most effective ways to develop yourself as a manager is to get a mentor whom you can model yourself on or to get a coach or coaches to support you through a variety of issues and challenges that you have. There is a reason why this works exceptionally well in the sports arenas. Fortunately, it is catching up in the business arena too....even in the UK!

3

N is for KNOW YOUR STAFF

> *"Friendship is born at that moment*
> *when one person says to another:*
> *"What! You too? I thought I was*
> *the only one""*
>
> C.S. Lewis

Here's a simple equation.
- There are 24 hours in a day and 168 hours in a week
- In the UK, the average person is at work from 9am to 5pm (i.e.8 hours a day), five days a week
- Most people have to commute to and from work (on average, 3 hours per day) and
- It is normal for most people to be at their places of work some 30 minutes before the official start time and stay a further 30 minutes after their official close time milling around, talking to colleagues, tidying up their desks, or as was the case in one of my places of work a few years ago, generally making sure that you are not the first person to leave the office, else it be interpreted as evidence of your lack of commitment!

This all adds up to 12 hours a day and 60 hours a week (i.e. 36% of the week) on work related matters.

If you factor in the fact that out of the 24 hours in the day, approximately 8 hours are spent sleeping, this means that on average we are awake for 112 hours a week and spend a whopping 54% of our weekly awake time on work related matters!

> To put it into perspective, most of us spend more time at work or on work related activities than we spend with our families.

Given that this is the case, how much do you really know your work colleagues? As a manager, how much do you really, *really* know about your staff members?

In case you are tempted to pat yourself on the back, please remember that each and every one of your staff members is more than just their daily work activities. So, what *else* do you know about, the people who spend more time delivering for you and making you look good than they do with their nearest and dearest?

If you are serious about developing your staff, you should make it your business to know about them, what makes them tick, their personal aspirations, why they make certain decisions, why they are currently over achieving / under achieving, their key family members etc etc. Get to know about the *real* and *whole* person in a genuine, interested and caring way and you will understand quickly about what "developing" means to them and the best way to support and assist them to be developed.

> Your people are much more than their careers

People are complicated. A favourite phrase in the UK, which always makes me laugh, is "*What you see is what you get!*". This is meant to describe the fact that a person is exactly the same as what they portray with their external demeanour. Indeed! I can honestly say that I have never met anyone who hasn't been much more than what I initially thought – either for better or for worse. That said, the best way that I have found to understand my staff over the years is to see them in the form of a triangle (Figure 4).

All the angles of the triangle have a direct impact on your people's performance at work and ultimately give you a better insight into possible development options which will be most relevant and tailored for them.

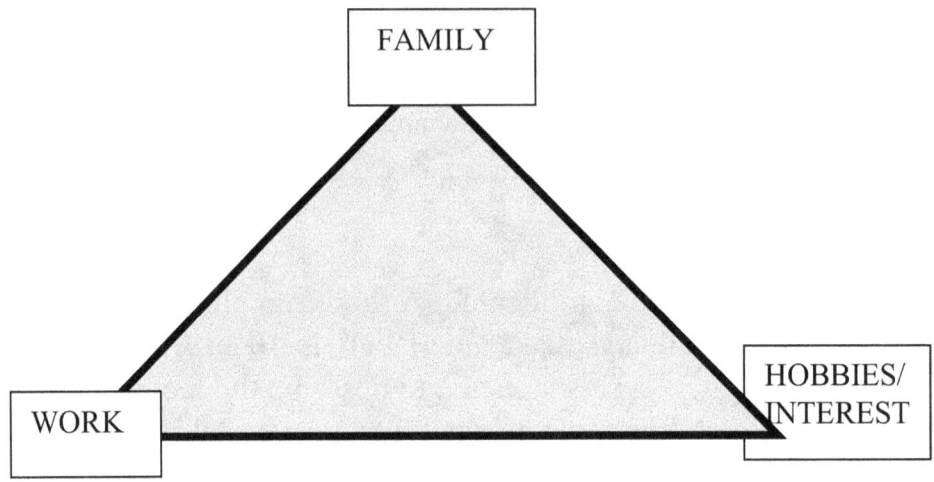

Figure 4 - The triangle of people development options

What's the relationship between WORK and developing people?

Hopefully, this is obvious. However, as a manager, please look beyond the obvious work/ tasks that your staff member is currently performing for you when you look to develop them. Why? This is because you may be surprised that where you logically see their career progression is not necessarily where they want to go. As such, any development intervention that doesn't take this into account will fail.

A few years ago, I had a very talented staff member in my team. Not only was he extremely good at the technical aspects of his job, he had exemplary behaviours and was an absolute pleasure to work with. He was going places. I identified him as a key talent for the future and enrolled him into my Function's Talent Management scheme[4] which was aimed at providing specific development opportunities and assignments for people to accelerate the realisation and maximisation of their potential. I was extremely excited for him and was looking forward to seeing him blossom.

To my surprise, he was less than enthusiastic about the prospect of being enrolled into the Talent Management pool. This was a prestigious honour and my colleagues felt that his lack lustre enthusiasm displayed some arrogance on his part.

They were wrong.

On speaking with him, I subsequently discovered that his hidden aspiration was to become a well respected Personal Trainer and that he had indeed been studying in the evenings for his Personal Trainer qualification and certification. Being enrolled into a Talent Management pool at work was only going to have a detrimental effect on his real aspirations and he clearly wasn't interested.

What's the relationship between FAMILY and developing people?

Often as a manager, you are required to make suggestions to your staff member about ways that they can improve

---

[4] Talent Management is discussed further in Chapter 7 of this book

their performance. Such suggestions may not necessarily be welcomed - especially if they don't feel that they had a gap or weakness in their performance in the first place. Using some sort of leverage or "in road" is a good way to gain their trust before they can feel comfortable enough to relax and see your point of view.

If you are a manager who knows and cares about the other elements of your staff's lives such as their family situation, their culture and their home responsibilities, and you care enough about them to enquire about these elements of their lives on occasions, you will find it easy to develop an effortless rapport and trust with them. In addition, you gain yourself a reputation as a manager who really cares - a "People Manager".

I have often given what I had assumed would be taken as bad or unwelcomed feedback to staff members about their performance, with some trepidation on my part, only to be pleasantly surprised that they agreed with me. As far as they are concerned, I am completely approachable and caring. So why therefore would I sabotage this reputation by giving advise which would be misleading or mischievous? Why indeed?

So, who would the average staff member take advise, feedback and criticism and suggestions from - a cold fish of a manager or a People Manager? If you are not seen as an effective People Manager, you are seriously jeopardising your abilities to develop your people and ultimately limiting the opportunities for them to deliver your organisation's objectives.

I suggest therefore that you do something about it fast and Chapter 2 has already provided some suggestions to explore in this area.

What's the relationship between HOBBIES/Interests and developing people?

I shall illustrate this with another story from my past.

Jacob[5] had a poor sickness and performance record. He had been moved in and out of various teams unsuccessfully and developed a reputation for unreliability and under performance. By the time he was assigned to my team, he was a lost cause and I was expected to performance manage him out of the organisation. I had my work cut out for me.

Through a series of one to one meetings and informal chats and coffees, I began to understand more about Jacob's interests outside of work. Eventually, the realisation dawned on me that:

- Jacob's sicknesses were, contrary to perception, actually genuine and
- His absences were as a result of repeated injuries he regularly sustained from his numerous intense extreme sports activities
- He wasn't eating properly either, and this coupled with frequent hectic sporting activities, contributed to his sustained injuries and poor health.

---

[5] For obvious reasons, this is not his real name.

I asked him to discuss the diet issue with his doctor, which he did. He was given a healthy Fitness and Diet plan which he was very happy to share with me. We frequently discussed his progress with following this and the challenges that he had. On the work front, I gave him specific and pivotal work objectives which he had to deliver within a strict timeframe as these were key enablers to other team members' abilities to deliver their own objectives. I also assigned him a mentor outside of my immediate team.

Jacob appreciated being assigned some "value-add" objectives especially as I made it clear that I knew that he was more than capable of delivering them successfully. Furthermore, he didn't want to let his peers down and he wanted to be seen as a pivotal member of a high performance team. He followed his diet plan, reduced his strenuous sports hobbies, got healthy and became more reliable. He has regular mentoring sessions with his mentor and developed a big brother/ little brother relationship with him which was charming. His sickness record reduced significantly as his motivation to perform at work increased. His performance improved so dramatically that people commented that it was a "flash by night" affair and that he was never going to sustain it. They were wrong. He sustained it and within a year was asking for significantly more stretching objectives.

Jacob was still in my team when I moved on and I happily handed him over, with pride, to my successor.

4

V is for REINVENT WITH THE TIMES

> *"In this world, nothing can be said to be certain, except death and taxes"*
>
> Benjamin Franklin

With respect, I disagree with Mr Benjamin Franklin on the above.
There are in fact three certainties in life - death, taxes and change!

Change is here to stay, so we need to make change an ally and embrace it. Continually developing people is one sure fire way to make change a friend. We can no longer sit on our laurels and expect that the skills which we developed and which have served us well over our careers will still remain relevant whilst everything around us changes. One only needs to take a look at so many of the job descriptions and roles which have sprung up over the last 5 years to see that skills and competency requirements are changing. There are for example, so many roles, positions and legitimate means of livelihood now which were virtually unheard of a few years ago. A colleague of mine recently told me of his son's friend who, after graduating from university, is employed by a major and serious multi-national organisation as an... "Ethical Hacker". His key role is to devote his time and energy legitimately devising the means and codes to break into his organisation's computer systems round the world - as a method of testing and securing the Company's security systems. Can you imagine what a cool job this is for someone who absolutely adores playing with computers? This sounds like fun, not work and most certainly, this type of activity/ work would have guaranteed a person a prison sentence a few years ago never mind a legitimate and lucrative means of livelihood.

So, what's my point? It is merely this. As a manager or leader, you owe it to your people to encourage them to reinvent themselves often and to refresh and / or develop new skills so as to strengthen their brand as the type of people with many strings to their bows. This is the most important way to stay relevant, motivated and gainfully employed doing the kind of things that gives you a buzz - regardless of whatever change is happening out there and regardless of whatever reorganisations are occurring.
In other words, you need to lead your people to emulate the great pop star Madonna - the queen of reinvention, who at the time of writing this, is No 1 on the UK Album charts with her 21st album ("MDNA"), some thirty years after she first emerged on the pop scene[6]. Indeed, I think it will be fair to say that Madonna has never left the entertainment industry and instead manages to find new and creative ways to gain and relate to an ever younger audience in spite of her 50+ years of age.

---

[6] Madonna's first record, titled Everybody, was released in 1982

As a manager, you need to encourage your staff to take up roles and assignments which will expand and stretch the boundaries of their comfort zones. These may be outside of their traditional skills and competencies and most certainly outside of their existing and comfortable teams.

An excellent senior mentor of mine once told me that every year she made it her duty to undertake a piece of assignment, activity or task which made her think *"Oh Sh#t - What have I let myself in for!"* As a development opportunity, she claimed that there was nothing like it and encouraged me to try it.
I did and still do and she was absolutely right.

One year, I left my *"Oh Sh#t!"* moment to December, the very last month of the calendar year to actually do it. It took me that long to pluck up the courage and my task of choice was to undertake a speaking engagement in front of a large and learned audience. I had to actively seek and volunteer myself for this gig and it didn't help that amongst the speakers for the event were people of far greater seniority than me with enviable job titles and status' to match. I did it. I received great feedback and new coaching clients and now I am hooked.

In terms of development and competencies, the ability to speak in public is currently one of the most highly regarded skills in Organisations and one of the most feared by individuals. I am not great at. There is definitely room for improvement. However, I am now very comfortable with it. Interestingly, more and more people now invite me to do speaking engagements and this has opened up further great opportunities for me.

"Opportunity is missed by most people because it comes dressed in overalls and looks like work" - Thomas Edison

Reinventing with the times is about being flexible and adaptable. Flexibility and adaptability are treasured competencies in today's work places. The willingness to try something new and challenging should be encouraged by managers. Too many people (and their managers) are married to inflexibility and this will ultimately be to their detriment. The world is changing. The workplace and the workforce are changing. Encourage your people to break their current static habit. Encourage them to change with the times and develop new skills in the process if they want to continue to be valuable both now and in the future. The days of solitary emphasis on linear progression are over. It is now about getting as much lateral development as possible. This is the way for people to develop and grow and continue to meet their businesses' needs and deliver to their businesses' bottom line.

"It is not the strongest of the species that survive, nor the most intelligent, but the one most responsive to change" - Charles Darwin

As a manager, you should make it your duty to provide as much reinvention opportunities, and engage in as much reinvention conversations, with your people as possible.

Be their coach as well as their Manager and help them to see the immense possibilities that they have to try something different and complimentary to what they already so. Incidentally, you should also try it yourself. I have a "two year rule" which means that every two years I have to engage in a new assignment, new project or work with a new team. With each piece of assignment, I consciously take stock of my transferrable skills and market this for a new role in an area where I have some gaps. At the end of a two year period in the new role, I would have closed the gaps which attracted me to that role in the first place and expanded my tool box of transferable skills for the next role.

I am not advocating that everyone embarks on a two year musical chair adventure like I do (and indeed it could be argued that there is something fundamentally wrong with me for seeking this frequency of change), but I do advise that people try something new as often as possible and more importantly, learn something new as often as possible.

Finally, I shall conclude this chapter by saying that in my opinion, not to find ways to reinvent yourself regularly with the times, either because of selfish reasons (see "*S is for Slavery is officially over*" chapter) or for fearful reasons, or indeed for any reason, is madness. A very wise and learned man is credited to have said that that madness is "*doing the same thing over and over again and expecting different results*" [7]. I couldn't agree more...especially in our ever changing economic climate.

---

[7] Albert Einstein

5

E is for EMPOWER YOUR PEOPLE .... and yourself

> *"He who throws a man down to the ground and proceeds to forcefully hold him down there with his own body, is also holding himself down"*
>
> Nigerian (Igbo) proverb

A manager who micro manages his staff in everything or every task that they do, is limiting their abilities to learn and develop and by so doing, also limits his own abilities to enhance his own performance. This is because the Manager is actually doing is supporting his staff to get to a stage where they are too afraid and/ or too inexperienced to be creative and think for themselves. As such, they become beholden to the manager for every decision.

For some managers and leaders, this element of control over their people is attractive as it means that their people do exactly what they are asked to and also limits the chances of any upstarts or "mavericks" sabotaging the manager's position and authority.

I empathise. There is nothing worse than a member of staff who suffers from delusions of grandeur and thinks that they know better than everyone else when in actual fact, they are "empty vessels"[8]. However, there can be absolutely no question that micro-managing, in every instance, is destructive. It prevents people from being developed and also says a lot (indeed too much!) about the insecurities and inefficiencies of the manager.

Empowering staff is a huge learning and development opportunity for both the staff and the manager alike. For the staff, it teaches them the key skill of responsibility, creativity, the ability to make and act on their own decisions, and more importantly, accountability. A staff member who is empowered thrives from the opportunity to make key decisions (based on research, analysis and subsequently, experience) and the accountability to stand by their own decisions, whether good or bad. Empowerment teaches staff members to raise their heads above the parapet and it eliminates the "slopey shoulders" syndrome.[9]

"I'd rather have 1% of the efforts of 100 people than 100% of my own efforts" - J. Paul Getty

---

[8] According to the popular adage, an empty vessel makes the loudest noise, hence my empathy!
[9] "Slopey shoulders" is a general term in used in predominantly large Organisations, whereby no one wants to make a decision for fear of being held accountable for it.

Empowerment is definitely great for staff members, however it poses big challenges for the manager.

One of the most important challenge is that the manager must quickly learn <u>how</u> and <u>when</u> to empower (preferably when the risks are relatively low) and most importantly, when to step in. Empowerment does not mean abdication on the part of the manager.

A manager who aims to become a great empowering manager, must develop some key opposing but complementary skills which will support him in empowering without abdicating.
These skills include marrying:

- Great interpersonal skills with the ability to make things happen and focus on results.
- Strategic skills (and ability to think Big Picture) with an analytical eye for detail so that they can quickly spot when a piece of work doesn't look or feel right.
- Supporting their team members and giving them "air cover" from senior management and outside criticisms, with giving detail and often unwelcome feedback and taking timely corrective actions face to face.
- The generous spirit to allow his people to make mistakes, with a clear and unmistakeable communication that the same mistakes will not be tolerated more than twice!
- Great relationship management and trust building skills with staff, with a personal focus to foster respect rather than likeability.

Empowerment frees both staff members and manager from the bondage of limitations and increases the motivations of both parties to carry on stretching themselves further to develop themselves quickly and more effectively.

As a manager, learn to develop your people by empowering them to take responsibility and accountability for their tasks, mistakes and successes.

Empowerment as a powerful motivating factor is also examined in Chapter 8 of this book.

6

S is for SLAVERY IS OFFICALLY OVER!

> *"Man is born free but everywhere he's in chains"*
>
> Jean Jacques Rousseau

Slavery is the flip side of the empowerment coin mentioned in the previous chapter. It's amazing how the average man abhors slavery with all his being and yet unwittingly participates in this despicable activity in the workplace. How is slavery practiced in the workplace?
Well, here are some scenarios:-

- When a Manager / Leader creates an atmosphere whereby his staff members are scared to express an interest in other internal opportunities outside of his team, but inside the organisation, in case they incur his wrath, this is slavery.
- When a manager shirks from his responsibility of performance managing his weak or incompetent staff, he is chaining them and the rest of the team to their incompetence. This is slavery.

- When a manager refuses to implement proactive succession plans for his department and his people, this is slavery.
- When a manager doesn't put as much emphasis into his staffs' personal development plans as he does to their operational plans/objectives, this is slavery.
- When a manager intentionally and deliberately and/or cowardly allows his staff to wallow in their delusions of grandeur regarding their technical and behavioural competencies, this is slavery.

As can be seen from my definitions of work slavery above, it can take many forms in the modern work place. Do not be a modern slave manager.

Do not hold on to your staff indefinitely in their roles either against their wills or against your better judgement. Instead, develop your staff by allowing them to explore and utilize the full spectrum of development opportunities. Help them to develop many strings to their bows (I have discussed this in the "V is for Reinvent yourself" chapter). This could include secondments to other departments, other organisations or indeed Sabbaticals.

If your staff are good performers, proactively plan for their exit (succession planning) and happily set them free with the confidence that there are other people whom you have developed to step into their shoes.

If your people are under performers, then assist them to find their strengths and talents and quickly & humanely set them free... to something that befits their skills and motivations. They might not thank you of course...but in the long run, if they are mature and you have handled this well, they will come to see that this was the best development opportunity that you could have given them.

Aim to be a responsible and ethical manager by regularly auditing and reviewing your staffs' key skills to do their jobs (the true definition of competency management) and help them to identify and plug their new skills/competency gaps.

Facilitate the implementation of your staffs' personal development plans and get them to actively own their own development. Support them wherever you can.

To conclude, developing your people to see and utilise a myriad of opportunities inside and outside your immediate team and, sometimes out of your organisation completely, is a practical acknowledgement of the fact that slavery (in any form) is indeed officially over.

Let's keep it that way please.

7

T is for TALENT MANAGEMENT

> *"My main job was developing talent. I was a gardener providing water and other nourishment to our top 750 people. Of course, I had to pull out some weeds too"*
>
> Jack Welch

The most popular definition of Talent Management is one which emphasises the strategic planning, recruitment, development and retention of a highly skilled workforce for an organisation or business.

There are many variations of the Talent Management process. Some organisations have a select Talent Pool with "highly talented" individuals whom they need to develop to take up key roles whilst other organisations go with the ethos that every individual has a talent but that the difference is the perceived relevance of the talent or skills to meet the changing needs of the organisation or business. I favour this latter definition because I *have to* assume that everyone was recruited into the organisation based on a perceived need of a perceived skill that they had. With this mind, the frequent review and assessment of your people's talents and the alignment of this with the changing objectives in your function or organisation or business is a key activity in developing people.

These are the key processes for Talent Management that all managers should actively lead on:

- Review, assess and re-assess your people's talents against actual performance and perceived potential for the future strategy of your Function/ Organisation
- Share, communicate and revise the talent assessment results with your people
- Adopt the most appropriate talent development intervention for your people

Review, assess and re-assess your people's talents against actual performance and perceived potential for the future strategy of your Function.

"I get to do what I like to do every single day of the year" - Warren Buffett

---

This activity starts with the premise that everyone has talents. However, as the goals and delivery objectives of business and organisation and its subsequent function and department change, some staff members may find that what they enjoy doing and therefore excel at, is no longer the crux of the department's objectives. As such, their actual performance begins to wane and their perceived potential to rise to the level to meet future organisation and departmental objectives, is limited.

The 9 box Talent Management[10] model (Figure 5) below is one of the most popular methods for assessing performance and potential.

Plotting staff on the Performance axis requires the transference of relevant performance management data from your performance or appraisal systems. I would recommend that that a manager aims to do this at least twice a year, adjusting positions on the graph as required to align with any changes in actual performance as required.

The assessment against the Potential axis is a more subjective one and therefore more difficult. To introduce as much objectivity into this assessment as possible, I would recommend that the manager incorporates as many views of the staff member's key stakeholders as possible and also that the manager develops a firm understanding of the strategic direction of his organisation or business and the key competencies and skills (leadership and technical) and experience deemed as being necessary to meet this vision.

---

[10] The 9 Box Model was introduced in 1957 by Igor Ansoff.

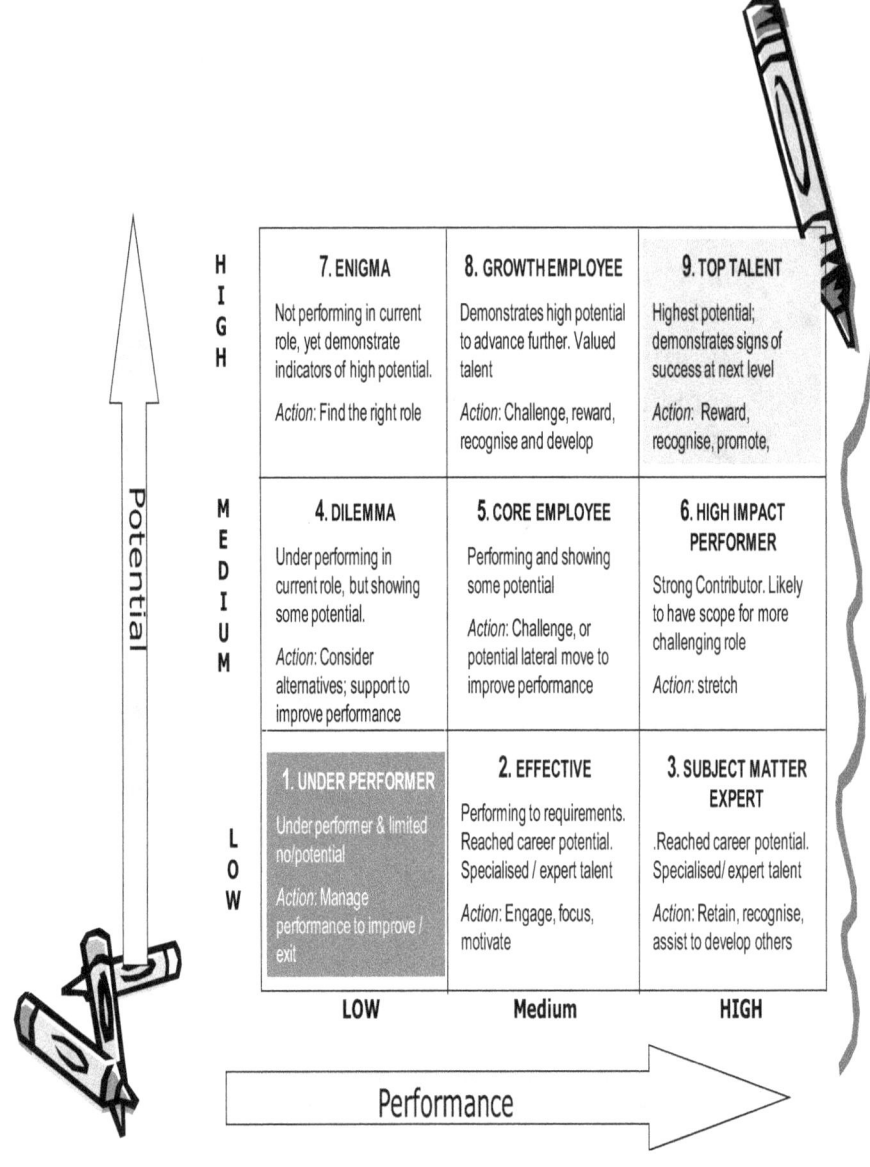

	LOW	**Medium**	**HIGH**
HIGH	**7. ENIGMA** Not performing in current role, yet demonstrate indicators of high potential. *Action*: Find the right role	**8. GROWTH EMPLOYEE** Demonstrates high potential to advance further. Valued talent *Action*: Challenge, reward, recognise and develop	**9. TOP TALENT** Highest potential; demonstrates signs of success at next level *Action*: Reward, recognise, promote,
MEDIUM	**4. DILEMMA** Under performing in current role, but showing some potential. *Action*: Consider alternatives; support to improve performance	**5. CORE EMPLOYEE** Performing and showing some potential *Action*: Challenge, or potential lateral move to improve performance	**6. HIGH IMPACT PERFORMER** Strong Contributor. Likely to have scope for more challenging role *Action*: stretch
LOW	**1. UNDER PERFORMER** Under performer & limited no/potential *Action*: Manage performance to improve / exit	**2. EFFECTIVE** Performing to requirements. Reached career potential. Specialised / expert talent *Action*: Engage, focus, motivate	**3. SUBJECT MATTER EXPERT** .Reached career potential. Specialised/ expert talent *Action*: Retain, recognise, assist to develop others

Potential (vertical axis)

Performance (horizontal axis)

Figure 5 – The Talent Management 9 box Model assessment

Share, communicate and revise the talent assessment results with your staff

"A man should never be appointed into a managerial position if his vision focuses on people's weaknesses rather than their strengths" - Peter Drucker

As a manager who is keen on developing his staff, it is vital that you share your analysis of their performance and potential with them. To make this meeting powerful and productive, I suggest that you take your staff through the talent assessment process, explaining that each of them have various talents and go through what types of talents /skills/ competencies and experience each of the talent boxes in **Figure 5** represents in your Organisation and why. You then invite them to tell you where they would place themselves on the grid and their reasons for doing so. Be open to the possibility of adjusting or revising your initial assessments (especially on the Potential axis) if required.

If you had been doing a good job with communicating and being open and honest with your staff all year round, the chances are that they would be very self aware regarding their position on the grid. Your role in the talent conversation is to steer them away from fixating on their weaknesses but on the alignment (or not) of their strengths to the new department objectives and vision and to agree on the best way forward.

Adopt the most appropriate talent development intervention for your people

"Remember, not even a machine is 100% efficient. Don't expect the humans who work for you to be" - The Mafia Manager

The most appropriate talent development intervention will depend on the position that the person has been assessed in the talent assessment grid and your ability to provide development opportunities to address the identified priority areas.

- Grids Nos 1, 4 &7 - people placed here need to improve their performance. The Manager should support them by finding the right assignment opportunities where the staff members can actively utilise their skills. In the case of the people within the red grid, this could very well be outside of your Organisation or Business. This may sound harsh, but ultimately, you truly are developing your team when you assist them to see that their underperformance in your team could be a simple case of a "square peg in a round hole" and the sooner they find the right fit for their skills and competencies the better.

- Grid Nos 2, 3 & 5 - represent people who need to manage their expectations. Develop your staff by encouraging them to articulate their career expectations and support them in finding ways to align these with your business/ function/

organisation's goals. Implement the right blend of learning opportunities (courses, on the job, mentoring, coaching, professional development etc) as required. Each case and each individual is different so please resist the temptation to throw money at a blanket development intervention for all.

- Grid Nos 6, 8& 9 - represent people who have performed very well and whose perceived future potentials to meet the changing needs of the organisation need to unlocked. The interesting thing about perceived potential is that if left untapped, it ceases to become potential. So stretch individuals by: (a) Putting them on succession plans for key positions in your department or business and empowering them with new stretching objectives and higher responsibilities and (b) Sharing information about their skills and career goals with other departments in your organisation and within your networks so as to extend the scope and boundaries of the development opportunities on offer. This may even mean engaging them on an external exchange secondment programme with likeminded businesses as you. This suggestion may seem counter-intuitive but it is a strategic thing to do for your business and yourself. It is the best way to retain talent (without enslaving them) and also has a huge potential to provide you with career opportunities in the future as you develop a reputation for yourself as an unselfish developer of people.

An altruistic talent management investment has boundless potential to be a profitable investment in the long run.

8

M is for MOTIVATE YOUR STAFF

> *"People often say that motivation doesn't last. Well, neither does bathing - that's why we recommend it daily"*
>
> Zig Ziglar

Motivating people is tough and often hit and miss! I say this from the standpoint of a person who has tried on so many occassions to motivate staff only to get it so very wrong. It would appear that I am not alone. Some Managers who have been involved in a Change, Transformation or Restructure programme have lamented the futility of their efforts to motivate their staff to engage with the change process or the outcome.

As mentioned in Chapter 2, people are motivated by either of two things: The gaining of pleasure or the the avoidance of pain and ultimately, our actions and decisions are based on our emotional (not logical) analysis of which activity will generate a <u>more</u> powerful feeling for us. With this mind, it is therefore unsurprising that scientists have concluded that most human beings will do more to avoid feeling pain (or what they percieve to be a pain) than to gain a pleasurable feeling.

For a manager trying to design and implement development activities for their staff based on what the manager perceives as pleasurable activities (e.g. Away days, team building activities, pub sessions, more responsibilities), this is a useful piece of information as it means that their good intentions may be viewed by some in their teams as leading to painful emotions, which, they will do all in their power to resist. To illustrate this point, I once delegated a new and high profile piece of assignment to a member of my staff (whom I shall call Angela) who was a star performer and who was seen as a potential high talent for the future. My intention in doing this was to provide a development opportunity which would stretch her competencies and skills further, increase her profile and get her noticed outside of my department and motivate her. I had absolutely no doubt that she would successfully deliver the assignment with the right support from me and so, I felt that the risk of such an assignment allocation was manageable.

On the contrary, the timing of my actions proved to be a high de-motivator for Angela. It was in January, there months to the end of our financial year and our annual Performance Review process. Angela perceived that the risk of her not doing this assignment well, and the possible effect on her annual Performance rating, was too much for her to take and therefore far outweighed the recognised development and career opportunity it would bring her if she performed as well as expected. I learnt a valuable lesson.

"Do not do unto others as you expect they should do unto you. Their tastes may not be the same" - George Bernard Shaw

Aligning the Pleasure/ Pain principle to the arena of motivation has taught me to motivate staff by concentrating on <u>removing or limiting the stuff which de-motivates</u> them and are therefore perceived as painful.

These are generally classified into the following:

- Lack of clear communications
- Lack of direction
- Lack of support or resources
- Lack of respect or fairness
- Lack of recognition
- Lack of empowerment or autonomy

Lack of clear Communications

This is a big potato. As such, I have dedicated **Chapter 12** exclusively to it.

Lack of Direction

A lack of direction causes nervousness on the part of staff members as it brings with it a lack of certainty. No one likes to feel uncertain about what they are doing, when and why. It is very demoralising.

As a manager, start with being clear with yourself about the goals and visions of your department or work function and communicate this to your staff constantly and through a variety of different media. Align each of your staff's individual objectives to your departmental goals so that they can clearly see the relationship between the tasks that they are being asked to do with the overall vision and objectives of the department and the organisation. Articulate to them how what they are doing is contributing to the Organisation's bottom line profitability. If there is a change in the strategic direction of your organisation, review and align their objectives accordingly so that they continue to remain relevant.

It is worth noting that if you are in a department or team which provides support services to the core business of your organisation, providing this direction or line of vision to the overall organisation objectives is particularly important for the development of your team. In my experience, people in support or back office or roles find that a lack of direction is one of their strongest de-motivating factors as it is harder for them to see how what they are doing is impacting the profitability of their organisation. As a manager, you have to pay particular attention to this aspect. Be brutal and begin with the end in mind. If what you are asking your staff members to do does not impact on the core business of the organisation, cut it out!

If you are uncertain about the direction of your organisation, due to a recent change, merger etc, please be honest with your staff and let them know that you do not currently have answer. However follow it up with a promise that once you are clearer (and by the way, make this soon), you would let them know what you know. Do not give them the impression that you are withholding information. This may make you sound important (i.e. one of the members of the inner senior management team) but it is detrimental to motivating your team.

Lack of Resources or Support

Resources here include tools, equipment, knowledge and of course management support. For every activity that you have given your staff to do, please agree with them the resources that they feel they will need to deliver the relevant results and make sure that they get this. A friend of a friend got her dream job in a male dominated construction industry. This was a win- win situation. She had been looking to break into the industry (but had always felt that her petite and feminine frame put her at a disadvantage) and the business itself had been looking to attract a more diverse workforce. Both parties were happy. The only problem was that the business hadn't accounted for the fact that whilst on a work site, their new female recruit would require a female toilet!

This is a perfect (albeit extreme) example of not having the resources to do the job.

Lack of Respect or Fairness

As a manager, remember that each one of your people craves respect. This could be in the way that you address them, talk to them, assign work to them, acknowledge their strengths and weaknesses and generally make them feel about themselves.

> "Everyone has an invisible sign hanging from their neck saying "*make me feel important*". Never forget this when working with people" - Mary Kay Ash

Treating people with respect means acknowledging that everyone is different and therefore you do <u>not</u> treat them equally, but fairly. This is a subtle difference in words but has a huge impact in motivating people. I fear that this subtlety between treating people fairly and treating them equally is being blurred and eroded in our quest to practice equal opportunities and as such is undoing all the good work that has been done around equality in the workplace over the past few years. As a manager, you need to respect your people by acknowledging their different needs and addressing these with the same amount of fairness for everyone. If this sounds confusing, let me illustrate by saying that bullying is a perfect example of a lack of respect. It should not be entertained under any circumstances. However, just because you have bullied Peter and Paul, is not a reason to also bully James, all in the name of treating them equally!

Lack of Recognition

A couple of quotations here will tell you the vital importance of recognising your people's capabilities and their achievements no matter how small, far better than I can.

"When people are placed in positions slightly above what they expect, they are apt to excel" - Richard Branson

"Everyone wants to be appreciated. So if you appreciate someone, don't keep it a secret" - Mary Kay Ash

When you recognise people, please be respectful and mindful of the context in which you are rewarding recognition. Awarding people with a certificate for "Employee of the Month" for example, against a backdrop when some of their colleagues are loosing their jobs following a restructure will be anything but motivating for either the recognised employee or their colleagues. It is an obvious point, I know. However, it is amazing how many managers, in their exuberance to be seen as motivating their people, end up doing just the opposite.

Lack of Empowerment or Autonomy

When a manager empowers their staff by delegating an important responsibility to them to manage and have responsibility and accountability for, the manager gives that person autonomy in the creative process and in the way they choose to deliver the required results or outputs. This sends a powerful message to the employee about how they are valued and in turn motivates them to deliver what is required and more. Not empowering your staff sends the complete opposite message to your staff and not only affects their performance but yours as a manager.

The importance of empowerment as a development tool has already been recognised in Chapter 5.

9

E is for EMPLOY THE RIGHT PEOPLE

> *"I hire people brighter than me and
> I get out of their way"*
>
> Lee Iacocca

Most times, a manager inherits a team and has to make the best of what he has. Occasionally, he gets the opportunity to engage new people either from within the organisation (especially if they are in a large enterprise) or from the external market place. Whether engaging from within or from outside of the Organisation, the same rule applies - "get the right people on the bus"[11].

This means:
- Resist the temptation to clone yourself!
- Engage people who have skills and competencies that are currently missing in your team (so that your existing team can learn from them)
- Engage people who have the right behaviours. Ideally they should also come "ready- made" with all the technical skills you need. However, if you have to trade off, I suggest that you go with the right

---

[11] Jim Collins: From Good to Great

behaviours as you can teach people skills but you cannot teach them to have a good attitude

By all means employ people who are more intelligent than you or your existing team but place more emphasis on emotional intelligence - i.e. people who have a highly developed sense of self awareness, self management, relationship management and social management competencies. A person who flies off the handle and behaves like a petulant child whenever any new change occurs or something doesn't go his way, is a bad influence on your team - and will send their development progress backwards. A person who bullies or talks down on other team members just because he is more technically competent than they are (or indeed for any reason), is a perfect example of a person with limited self awareness, self management and emotional intelligence and therefore should not be employed. Even if, you find that you have made a mistake and hired them (let's face it, only a fool will display their undesirable tendencies at the interview stage), act quickly and stamp this out or stamp them out!

Engage people from a wide variety of backgrounds and demographics not because it is a politically correct thing to do in this age of diversity in the workplace but because it makes perfect business and bottom-line profitability sense. Diversity in a team promotes more creativity, more business awareness, more customer awareness (after all, I would hazard a guess that your customers are from a cross section of demographics), more opportunities for development of interpersonal skills and a higher ability to make things happen.

Working with diversity therefore, provides a great development opportunity for your people.

To promote diversity in your team and business, I would recommend the following:

- Review where and how you advertise for staff. Are you inadvertedly excluding a particular section of talent because of your chosen medium of advertisement?
- Employ people with transferable skills who have worked in a variety of positions which may not necessarily be the traditional career progression that you would expect. The current preoccupation to engage someone who has done the same role for ever as the perfect example of a person with experience, is I submit, outdated and myopic. Ask yourself: Has the person got 10 years experience of one role or have they got 1 year's experience of 10 roles?
- Encourage diversity in personality types and social styles in your team. Use the Bolton and Bolton Personality styles grid[12] in Figure 6 below to assess the range of personality types you have in your team, their strengths and their weaknesses and the best way for them to work with, and communicate with each other – as well as their learning styles.

---

[12] Derived from People Styles at Work: Making Bad Relationships Good and Good Relationships Better - Robert Bolton & Dorothy Bolton

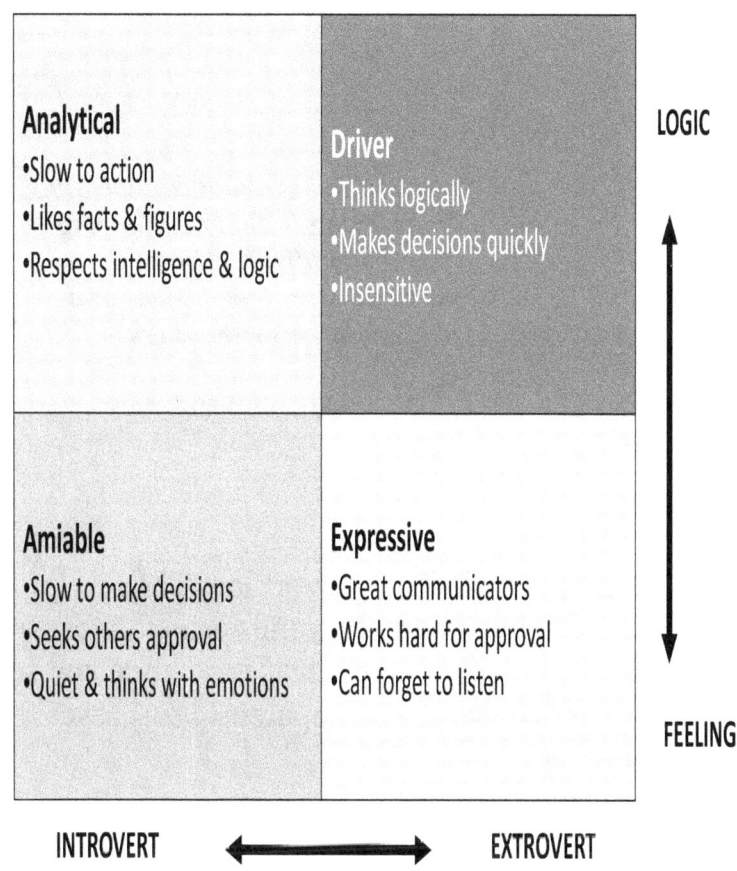

Figure 6 - Diverse Personality Styles

10

N is for NETWORK, NETWORK, NETWORK!

> *"Networking is about connecting. Networking is about enhancing your own individual potential by sharing knowledge, ideas and resources with others"*
>
> Andy Lopata

Most people dislike networking. The fear of rejection is always forefront in our minds as is the fear of making total fools of ourselves. This fear is so huge and so disproportional that it apparently surpasses the fear of dying[13].

No matter our fears, networking is a huge development tool. The theory of six degrees of separation created by Professor Stanley Milgram in 1967, states that we are only six steps away from anyone in the world. Think about the possibilities of this with regards to access to resources for developing your people and yourself.

---

[13] Andy Lopata in his book "...And Death Came Third" refers to a survey in which people stated their worst fears, in order to be (1). Networking; (2). Public Speaking; and (3). Fear of dying

In Chapter 7, "T is for Talent Management", I alluded to the importance of selling your staff's achievements or sharing information about their skills and career goals across your networks so as to extend and attract more high profile and meaningful development opportunities for them. Networking provides the platform and mechanism for doing just this and thanks to the theory of six degrees of separation, a manager's ability to network successfully has become one of the most important avenues for developing both his staff....and himself.

Key skills and competencies that are developed and/or enhanced through the networking approach include:
- Communication
- Influencing
- Stakeholder Management
- Relationship Management
- Ability to think creatively and think on your feet
- Searching for information
- Understanding Others
- Building Confidence
- Building Teams
- Increasing your profile
- Business/ Industry knowledge

This is not bad for starters. In addition, it is worth remembering that these skills are all intensely transferrable from one job to the other and from one role to another. They also enhance your promotional prospects as it has become one of the most open secrets today that promotions are given not on the basis of a person's performance alone but on the basis of how much is known about them - and who their business cheerleaders or supporters are.

Having spent my formative management years expecting, with limited success, that my unsung performance will somehow speak for me when it comes to attracting new opportunities and promotions, I now know better. I have forced myself to become a better networker. I do not find it particularly easy but I find it absolutely necessary. Most of the opportunities that I have had over the past few years have come to me via my networks...and that includes the idea to write this book.

Networking is not to be sneezed at. The good news is that more of us are scared of this than are confident. There is therefore unity in numbers when it comes to apprehension. Always remember that you are not alone ...and it is for a worthy cause.

Encourage your staff to do as much networking as possible. They will be scared but explain that you are too and that Rome wasn't built in a day. Support them. Start with making it a point to get yourself invited to some of the informal events that your Business has or that other teams are involved in. Go with your staff member and introduce them to some people that they don't know and take it from there.

In addition, encourage them to register with business social networking sites such as LinkedIn, and advice that they join some of the groups which may be of particular interest and actively contribute to their discussions. As well as networking with other members. They also have a great opportunity to learn something new.

I shall conclude this topic with a little story.

www.facilitate4me.com

One of my networks recently introduced me, via email to a very powerful person in his networks whom he felt could support me in a new venture that I wanted to embark on. I booked a meeting to see this powerful person (whom I shall call Pamela), and was so nervous about making the right impression that I literally rehearsed and visualised every aspect of my meeting with her beforehand. My meeting with Pamela went extremely well and I was surprised and delighted with how open and warm she was and also with how generous she was with her advice. One of the "home works" that she left me with was that I had to network more and she suggested a particular business group which she felt would be ideal. Up to that time, I hadn't even heard of such a group. Pamela mentioned a forthcoming seminar that the group was scheduled to hold and suggested that I should attend. Needless to say, I was petrified. Taking advantage of her warmth and generosity, and thinking on my feet, I admitted my fear and asked if I could tag along with her when she went. She was more than happy to say Yes and a week to the date, her PA contacted me to ask if I was still up for it and if I had purchased my ticket for the event. I hadn't...but I did immediately.

The evening before the event, Pamela emailed me with her apologises. Due to some unforeseen circumstances at work, she was now unable to attend. She however wanted me to go ahead and attend without her.

I could have ducked out, and indeed, I wanted to, but something told me that I had to be courageous and committed. I also felt that perhaps this was her way of testing my resilience and commitment[14]. I attended the event and thoroughly enjoyed it. I also made a valuable new contact. I reported back my experience to Pamela and her delight at me was obvious. It was almost as if she was saying to me ...*You see, I knew you could do it*!

It felt great!

---

[14] Resilience and commitment are two very important qualities for anyone wishing to get the most out of networking!

11

T is for THINK CREATIVELY

> *"Not everything that counts can be counted and not everything that can be counted counts"*
>
> Albert Einstein

Developing people is one of the most important activity that a manager or leader needs to perform. However, when times are hard, developing people takes a back seat as the emphasis turns to the more tangible activities and quick wins that drive the bottom line profitability.

The crux of the matter is that great people drive the bottom line and great people are developed by managers and leaders just like you. Not developing your people therefore makes bad economic sense and the conclusion of the CMI[15] survey in the Introduction of this book makes that very clear. What's a manager to do then?

The answer is that managers need to be creative as to how to put some tangible and financial benefits to the People Development agenda in their business and also on how to

---

[15] The Chartered Management Institute.

measure the return on their investment. Deliberately omitting to do this is akin to throwing latent investments into the toilet or washing them down the drain. Remember, the CMI *conservatively* estimates that £19billion is lost every year in the UK from symptoms of not developing people. If your business is in the UK, ask yourself how much of this £19billion can be apportioned to the lack of people development in your business/ team/ function/ organisation. If your business is not in the UK, don't think that you are exempted. Ask yourself the same question. How much is your business loosing by not investing in developing your people? More importantly, what can you do about it?

The answer is that you need to think creatively.

Thinking creatively is about:
- You translating people development into bottom line figures so as to truly understand why this is important to your business and ultimately, your success as a manager. **Table A** below gives you my interpretation of the overall formula that I believe was used by the CMI to get to the £19 billion figure. Apply the same equation to your business and see for yourself how that translates to your workplace. Then you can use this amount that you are pouring down the drain (because that is clearly what it is) to grab the senior management attention in your business and start to influence the people that matter

- Not being overwhelmed about developing people but finding the right and often bespoke solutions that work for your business. Please note that there is no "one size fits all" answer to what works. What works for Business A may not necessarily work for Business B because the people's strengths and development areas may be different in both businesses and your business goals and priorities may also be different. You need to do the analysis and as shown in the chapter on *"T is Talent Management"*, you need to find what works specifically for <u>you.</u>

- You as a manager being open and honest about which aspects of developing people is or isn't your forte <u>and</u> doing something about it. The most important role that a manager has is to develop his people and yes, you are a manager and the accountability for people development rests with you. However, there is no rule on earth that says that you have to do it *yourself.* If you don't enjoy it or don't feel that you have the time or skill for it, it is most important that you recognise this and then hire, engage, outsource or delegate to the right people who can support you by delivering the development on your behalf. This delegation (not abdication) could be to people within your organisation or business or outside. It doesn't really matter. The most important thing is for you to get them, make sure that you give them the correct brief regarding your requirements and that you ensure that people development is being done. Your initial reaction could be that employing the services of an external people developer or engaging in outside development intervention will be expensive. This is a valid concern. My response to it is this: now that you have hopefully worked out how much you are throwing down the drain by not developing people, can you really afford to throw more down the drain by half heartedly embarking on a development exercise or running the risk of wasting more money by not doing it well? You need to see if your business case warrants the extra expense. If it does, then go for it and convince your bosses that it makes economic sense to do this in this creative way. If the business case doesn't stack up, then try something else.

What is your Business' share of the £19billion loss per year?

My interpretation of the CMI formula is that it is based on 75% of employees in a business earning an average of £9.00 an hour wasting 2 hours each week every year due to their Manager's unclear communication, lack of support, micro-management and lack of direction.

So if your business has 100 staff:
- 75% of 100 staff = 75 people
- 2 hours loss per week for the staff = 75 staff x 2 hours = **150 hours/ week**
- Average working weeks in a year = 48 weeks
- Average hours lost by all employees per year in the Business = 48weeks x 150hours = **7,200 hours**)
- At a salary of £9.00/ hour = 7,200 hours x £9.00 =

£64, 800

Table A – How much are you loosing from bad management practices?

12

And not forgetting to...COMMUNICATE, COMMUNICATE, COMMUNICATE!

> *"To effectively communicate, we must realise that we are all different in the way we perceive the world and use this understanding as a guide to our communication with others"*
>
> Anthony Robbins

To communicate effectively with your staff is to develop them. The Association of Project Managers (APM) Body of Knowledge, 5th Edition defines Communication as *"the giving, receiving, processing and interpretation of information"*.

 I started off the Introduction section of this book with a reference to the CMI survey on bad managers and the symptoms of bad management. Interestingly, all the worst management practices highlighted in the survey reflected in some form or the other, elements of giving, receiving processing and interpreting of information i.e. direct or perceived communication.
For example:

- *"Unclear communication"* - refers to the giving and processing of information
- *"Lack of Support"* - refers to processing and interpreting of information
- *"Micro management"* – refers to interpreting of information
- *"Lack of direction"* - refers to giving and receiving of information
- *"Lack of communication"* - refers to giving of information

---

"Communication is everyone's panacea for everything" - Tom Peters

---

From my experience, the biggest complaint that employees have about "management" seems to centre on communication. However, it has also been my experience that when pushed to elaborate further, no two employees ever agree on what effective and consistent communication looks like. This means that ultimately, any piece of communication, no matter how well crafted or well intentioned is open to misunderstanding by someone if they so choose.... or in some cases, unwittingly. This is scary.

Some time ago, I led the people work stream of an organisation restructure change programme which had a lot of implication on people. Naturally people were nervous of the implications of outcome on themselves ...and suspicious. No matter how hard my team and I tried to ensure that all the stakeholders were communicated to in

the most appropriate manner, at the right time and with the right information, the grapevine machine worked overtime with insinuations and counter insulations aimed at supposedly dissecting our every move. Every written piece of communication from my team was over analysed by certain sections of the community, every body language was interpreted and misinterpreted and every omission, no matter how innocent, was used as fodder to feed the rumour mill and presented as proof of a lack of openness and transparency on our part. Indeed one particular piece of the misinterpretation was so fantastic and impressive, albeit completely off the mark, that I was forced to rebut it (in frustration) with an *"it couldn't possibly be true as my intelligence does not stretch that far"* remark.
I was damned if I did and damned if I didn't.
 I learnt a valuable lesson.

There is no such thing as a 100% proof communication.

The effectiveness of a piece of communication depends, to a large extent, on the processing abilities and the perceptions of the receiver. We all process and perceive information in different ways dependent on our experience and reference points, therefore, we will all react differently to the same piece of communication.

As a manager, my advice is that you should remember this whenever you want to communicate to your people and don't expect that all of them will "get it" first time around. Instead aim to think about the following key points:

1. Err on the side of over–communicating rather than under-communicating as people tend to read too much into any perceived communication vacuum.

However, once you start on the path of over-communicating, make sure you continue as failure to remain consistent will be detrimental and give your people an unwelcome opportunity to over analyse... and get it wrong.

2. Before embarking on a piece of communication, begin with the end in mind. Be absolutely clear about your objectives and most importantly, what actions and emotions you want your communications to invoke in your people. Once you know this, then you can start to design and structure your communication taking care to adequately craft it in such a way as to engage with the key senses of your audience.

3. Use what you know about your people (From **"N is for Know your People"** chapter) to tailor the communication accordingly. Avoid the temptation to do a "one size fits all" type of communication and cram many objectives and many styles into one. So, when giving out work instructions or work directions, practice what I call "Situational Communications" which requires you to apply the most relevant communications style and medium for the message at hand.

4. Acknowledge that communication is a two way process, and make every effort to also listen to your people. Make sure too that you are <u>seen</u> to have acted upon any of their recommendations which you have agreed to implement.

5. Pick up on what is said by your people and more importantly, on what isn't said. Learn to read and interpret people's moods and what a change in their mood indicates. On the latter, clearly you are not telepathic, so it would make sense for you to ask them

6. Speaking about asking questions, learn to do this in a most sensitive and unthreatening or non accusatory manner. Ask questions like you are genuinely interested[16] in the response and not as if you want to put them on the stand in court. Choose your words carefully and adjust your tone appropriately so as not to give the impression that your aim is to gather evidence to use against them at a future date[17].

7. Be accessible to your people. This is particularly important if your workplace is going through a change. Don't hide behind your desk and don't hide behind your headphones...even if it is an acceptable piece of equipment in your office. Do not change the route in which you normally enter your office building, in an attempt to avoid people or avoid questions. Human beings are generally regarded as creatures of habit and as such people will notice when your usual habits change particularly in times of uncertainty. I was recently told the story of a Manager who, during a period redundancy for a large number of his workforce, suddenly developed an insatiable urge to use the stairs, instead of the lifts, to get to his desk on the 7th floor of the office

---

[16] For example: "What are the factors which contributed to your late arrival today?"
[17] For example: "Why are you late again?"

building. He told people that he wanted to increase his fitness levels but everyone knew that this was an ill disguised ploy to avoid seeing the usual crowd in the lifts and being forced to answer some difficult questions about their uncertainty for the future. I always think that "walking the floor" is one of the best ways to communicate with people as you get to speak with your people about what really matters to them at work in an informal manner and in their own environment. This strips away any need for them to display any airs and graces around you and has the added advantage of making you appear more "user - friendly."

8. Be open to receiving both good news and bad news - especially the bad news. Please resist any temptation to "shoot the messenger" as the ability of your staff to communicate bad news to you is definitely a huge progress in the two way- communication process and implies trust. It also means that you get an early visibility and "heads up" of when things *look* as if they are *likely* to go wrong and therefore need your corrective intervention, instead of at the point when the s**t *actually* does hit the fan!

9. Give and ask for feedback from your people – and use the latter constructively to develop yourself to be a better People Manager. Years ago a very clever colleague of mine was vehemently opposed to asking or receiving any feedback from her staff as she saw this as undermining her status as their Manager and therefore demeaning. The result was a breakdown of open and honest two way communication and a complete lack of trust on the part of her team. They

viewed some of the excellent initiatives which she instigated for their development, with suspicion and even though they made the right noises in front of her, behind her, there was a total lack of engagement and buy-in. This was a real shame for her ideas were brilliant.

10. Explain the reasons why you are developing or implementing any new initiatives or new ways of working. Create a real sense of urgency and aim to package your intervention as a move away from any of their pressing pains or bugbears. This should go a long way towards the adoption and implementation of your initiative. Engage a small team of key and credible (by their peers) opinion formers to get behind this initiative so that they can also sell and spread the word to their colleagues. Some time ago my team and I developed a Competency Framework for a community of 600 staff in our function. This required staff to honestly assess their skills and competencies against the guidelines provided so that we could objectively analyse their skills gaps and address this. We were very aware of the suspicion that would follow such an exercise especially if perceived as a tool for assessing performance or appraising staff. We resisted the temptation to elevate ourselves to the position of "experts" on what the various competencies should be and instead, engaged a core group of respected, opinionated and experienced people from within the community to work with us on this project. Their inclusion on the project created a certain ownership in their minds which translated to their willingness to "sell" the value- add of the finished Competency

Framework product and processes to their colleagues. They also played a fantastic role in dispelling any uncertainty about any perceived undesirable motives behind this project and change initiative.

To conclude, investing in a robust, flexible and timely communication process is a complex but necessary activity as it is clear that communications envelope the whole developing people package. Its usefulness therefore cannot be over emphasised. Likewise, the potential and impact of getting it wrong cannot be under played.

The final word on this is aptly summarised in the following quote:

"Communication is a skill that you can learn. It's like riding a bicycle or typing. If you are willing to work at it, you can rapidly improve the quality of every part of your life" - Brian Tracy

13

Conclusion

"In short whoever you may be,
To this conclusion you'll agree,
When everyone is somebodee,
Then no one's anybody"

William Shakespeare

The whole premise of this book has been to emphasise that within the business arena, people matter.

As a manager, your people are not *just* anybody whom you can ignore and mismanage at will, but incredible resources that require the right investments so as to get the best out of the them. Everybody in your team is somebody...but then I think you already you know this else you would not have invested in reading this book.

Great people are developed by great managers.

The chances are that when it comes to developing your people, everything in this book is common sense. The chances are also that not everything is this book is *always* followed by your managers or the managers around you. So, here is your opportunity to buck the trend. There would have been certain chapters in this book that particularly resonated with you for a variety of business or personal reasons. It is now your opportunity to use the broad guide provided, combine with your experience and your priority to really start the tailored development of your people and yourself.

As you embark and continue with this journey, please remember the following key things:

Developing people is about making the right INVESTMENT whereby:

- I is for ....Invest in yourself
- N is for .... kNow your staff
- V is for .... reinVent with the times
- E is for ....Empower your people....and ultimately yourself
- S is for .... Slavery is officially over!
- T is for............Talent Management
- M is for..........Motivate for people
- E is for ....Employ & Engage the right people
- N is for ....Network, Network, Network!
- T is for .... Think Creatively

The most important role that a manager has is to develop his people, however, there is no rule on earth that says that you have to do it JUST by *yourself.* Make use of all the resources around you and if you feel that I can provide any support to you, please feel free to contact me via www.faciliate4me.com

BIBLIOGRAPHY

1. About.com: Human Resources - Susan M Heathfield
2. …And Death Came third – Andy Lopata & Peter Roper
3. APM Book of Knowledge - 5th Edition
4. Awaken the Giant Within - Anthony Robbins
5. Emotional Intelligence - The New Leaders - Daniel Goldberg
6. From Good to Great - Jim Collins
7. It's the People! - John A. Dembitz
8. Managing in times of Change - Michael Maggin
9. People's Styles at Work: Making Bad Relationships Good and Good Relationships Better - Robert Bolton & Dorothy Bolton
10. Personnel Today: Bad Management costing billions - John Eccleston
11. Talk your way to the top - Kevin Hogan

www.ingramcontent.com/pod-product-compliance
Lightning Source LLC
Chambersburg PA
CBHW081554170526
45166CB00009B/2697